DAYS THAT SHOOK THE WORLD

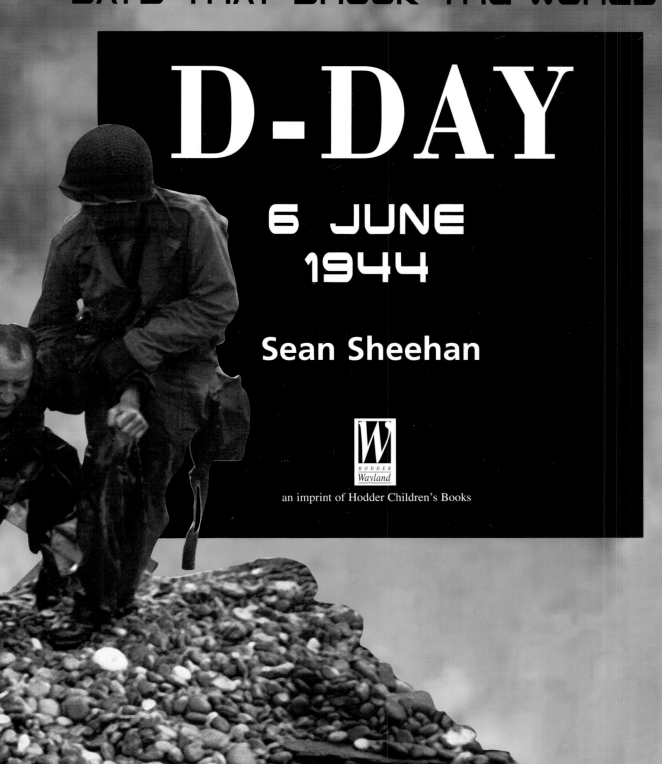

D-DAY

6 JUNE 1944

Sean Sheehan

HODDER
Wayland

an imprint of Hodder Children's Books

DAYS THAT SHOOK THE WORLD

Assassination in Sarajevo	The Dream of Martin Luther King
D-Day	The Fall of the Berlin Wall
Hiroshima	The Kennedy Assassination
Pearl Harbor	The Moon Landing
The Chernobyl Disaster	The Wall Street Crash

Produced by Monkey Puzzle Media Ltd
Gissing's Farm, Fressingfield
Suffolk IP21 5SH, UK

First published in 2002 by Hodder Wayland
An imprint of Hodder Children's Books
Text copyright © 2002 Hodder Wayland
Volume copyright © 2002 Hodder Wayland
This paperback edition published in 2003

Series Concept: Liz Gogerly
Design: Jane Hawkins
Editor: Patience Coster
Picture Researcher: Lynda Lines
Consultant: Michael Rawcliffe
Map artwork: Michael Posen

Cover picture: As an Allied landing craft nears the Normandy beaches, soldiers wade ashore under heavy machine-gun fire (Corbis/Robert F Sargent).
Title page picture: American soldiers help their comrades at Utah beach (Corbis/Weintraub).

We are grateful to the following for permission to reproduce photographs:
AKG Photo 7 bottom, 19, 38 top; The Art Archive/National Archives 6, 9, 16 top, 34; Associated Press 41; Bettmann/Corbis 7 top, 10, 11 bottom, 12, 13, 30 left, 32, 35 top, 39; Camera Press Ltd 17 (Imperial War Museum), 27 (Imperial War Museum), 33 (Imperial War Museum), 36 (Yevgenny Khaldei); Corbis 15 (Kurt Hutton), 18 (Moore), 22 (Robert F Sargent), 23 top, 23 bottom (Weintraub), 26, 28, 31, 40 (Robert Maass), 42 (Dave G Houser), 43 (Owen Franken), 46 (Michael John Kielty); Hulton-Deutsch Collection/Corbis 8, 11 top, 16 bottom, 20, 21, 25, 29 bottom, 30 (right), 35 bottom; Press Association/Topham 24; Topham 14, 29 top, 37, 38 bottom.

Printed and bound in Italy by G. Canale & C.Sp.A., Turin

British Library Cataloguing in Publication Data
Sheehan, Sean, 1951-
D-day. - (Days that shook the world)
1.World War, 1939-1945 - Campaigns - France - Normandy - Juvenile literature
I.Title
940.5'42142

ISBN 07502 3568 3

Hodder Children's Books
A division of Hodder Headline Limited
338 Euston Road, London NW1 3BH

CONTENTS

At sunrise on 6 June 1944, in the channel of sea separating England from Normandy in France, an extraordinary moment in history is about to begin. Countless ships carrying many thousands of armed soldiers plough their way through the choppy, grey waves. Other ships sail alongside, transporting heavyweight weapons like tanks and artillery; further ships contain jeeps, lorries, ammunition, and supplies of food and provisions. They all share a common destination – a fifty-mile stretch of coast and its five sandy beaches on the northern coast of France.

The soldiers on board know that enemy troops are waiting to try and kill them when they land. They know too that today is 'D-Day', and that everything hangs on this, the critical start to a planned invasion of Nazi-occupied Europe. The combined armies of the Allies, those countries at war with Germany, will attempt to wrest back control of western Europe and begin to bring about the hoped-for end to the Second World War.

The ships left the English coast in silent darkness during the very early hours of the morning. Not until they were on board ship and heading for France were the commanding officers allowed to open the sealed envelopes containing maps and details of the precise role they and their troops were to play on D-Day. Now, as dawn breaks, Allied bombers are seen flying overhead, and the sound of enemy fire can be heard from the German positions above the beaches. Plumes

At a port in southern England a truck reverses on to a US landing craft. This means that it will be in the correct position to drive off on to a beach in Normandy on D-Day.

of black smoke rise up from ships and landing craft hit by enemy shells, while streaks of fire and smoke burst from the sides of battleships as they pound the shore with their huge guns. High up the beach, the soldiers can see flashes of light and hear the sound of mortar shells exploding. Standing, sitting, crouching, the soldiers wait in the ships. Many are suffering terribly with seasickness. They are mostly silent. The soldiers' thoughts turn to home – how many of them will return after D-Day?

Out at sea, the big ships come to a halt, and the men clamber into the flat-bottomed landing craft hanging from the sides of the ships. Aboard these small boats the soldiers will approach the beaches. The large ships turn about to make the return journey to England for more troops. As the soldiers wait for the ramp to drop down at the front of the landing craft, they know that there is only one choice open to them. Under enemy fire from machine guns in defended positions above the beach, they must wade through the shallow water and out on to the land.

These Canadian troops packed into an assault craft can only sit and wait as they approach the Normandy coast.

This poster commemorating D-Day shows the international nature of the operation.

How Many Came Back?

" We had soldiers living just across the road from us. They were warned not to talk to civilians, but the officers in charge turned a blind eye and we were invited to join them for a drink on the night before they were due to leave. The officers had given them a barrel of beer and they asked me if I would bake for them and gave me all the ingredients, much more than I needed. That evening we had a lovely time, the men were singing and drinking.... We, and about three other couples, were up at dawn to see them go. We waved till they were out of sight, me with tears streaming down my face. They left before I could make them the cake and I knew they had found this way of just giving me very rare rations. I often wonder how many of them came back. "

Marjorie Box from Hampshire in the south of England remembers soldiers leaving for D-Day. Quoted in Nothing Less Than Victory by Russell Miller.

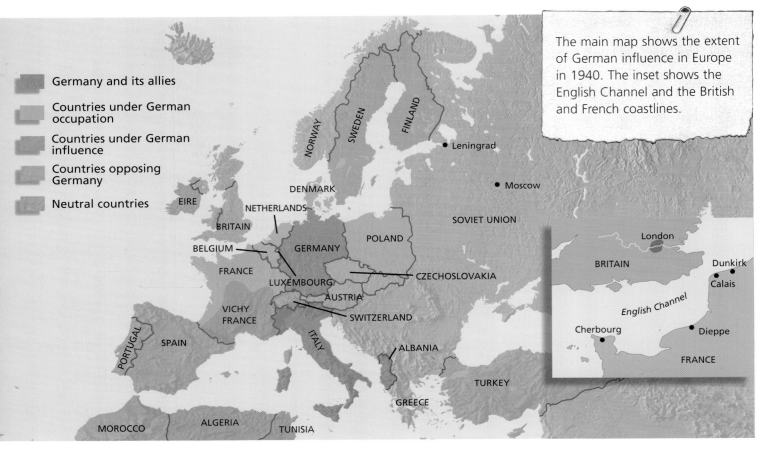

Germany and its allies

Countries under German occupation

Countries under German influence

Countries opposing Germany

Neutral countries

The main map shows the extent of German influence in Europe in 1940. The inset shows the English Channel and the British and French coastlines.

NORWAY
SWEDEN
FINLAND
Leningrad
DENMARK
Moscow
NETHERLANDS
EIRE
BRITAIN
SOVIET UNION
BELGIUM
GERMANY
POLAND
FRANCE
LUXEMBOURG
CZECHOSLOVAKIA
AUSTRIA
VICHY FRANCE
SWITZERLAND
PORTUGAL
SPAIN
ITALY
ALBANIA
TURKEY
GREECE
MOROCCO
ALGERIA
TUNISIA

London
BRITAIN
Dunkirk
Calais
English Channel
Cherbourg
Dieppe
FRANCE

THE ARMADA OF MEN, ships, weapons and provisions that made its way to France on 6 June 1944 faced the challenging task of taking on a Nazi Germany that controlled most of Europe. The Second World War had started in 1939 when Germany invaded Poland and Britain responded by declaring war on Germany. In less than twelve months, Adolf Hitler's Nazi regime had conquered some 250 million Europeans. Even before war broke out, Austria and Czechoslovakia (now the two countries of the Czech Republic and Slovakia) had come under German domination. At the start of the war, Hitler had conquered Poland in less than a month. Other countries were overrun even more swiftly: Norway within weeks, Denmark and Luxembourg within a day. Then followed the defeat and occupation of the Netherlands and Belgium and, within six weeks, the surrender of France. In 1940, 200,000 British and 120,000 French troops were evacuated in an emergency

The German leader Adolf Hitler (at the front, second from right), seen here on a visit to German-occupied Paris, France in 1940.

A Moment in Time

Japan is an emerging military power in the East. Germany's decision to attack the Soviet Union gives Japan the resolve she needs to assert herself in Asia. In the early hours of 7 December 1941, Japanese aircraft attack the American naval base at Pearl Harbor in Hawaii. In less than two hours, the Japanese have sunk or disabled nineteen ships, destroyed 120 aircraft and killed 2,400 people. The United States is not prepared for war and presents Germany with no immediate threat. However, on 8 December, the USA declares war on Japan. On 11 December, Germany and Italy, Japan's allies, declare war on the USA.

Bombs rain down on the US naval base at Pearl Harbor.

operation at Dunkirk in northern France, where they were forced to flee from the advancing German army.

The scale and pace of these conquests had turned Nazi Germany into a powerful empire and an economic superpower. The Nazis, ruling as a dictatorship, set out to create a new European civilization based on what they believed to be their racial superiority. (They regarded Jews, Slavs, gypsies and other groups of people as racially inferior.) But to continue their conquest of Europe, the Nazis needed to invade Britain, an island separated from the European mainland by just 34 kilometres (21 miles) of sea. Hitler set about this task in the summer of 1940 when the German air force, the Luftwaffe, attempted to destroy the British Royal Air Force (RAF). If Britain no longer had an air force with which to defend itself, Germany could invade confidently and speedily.

However, the Luftwaffe was unable to defeat the RAF. The struggle between them for control of the skies became known as 'the Battle of Britain'. Hitler's failure to defeat the RAF did not concern him unduly.

Although Britain had resisted invasion, Hitler knew that the island was isolated in Europe and lacked the means with which to attack the mainland. Hitler decided to postpone his conquest of Britain; he would return to this problem, but had a more important enemy to deal with first. If the Soviet Union could be conquered, Hitler believed, Nazism would emerge as a world power and Britain would soon be brought to heel.

Hitler had always regarded the communist-led Soviet Union as Germany's natural foe, and Britain as its natural ally. He admired Britain's sea-based empire, and had courted Britain with a view to dividing the world between the two countries.

In 1941, the USA joined forces with Britain after Japan, Germany's ally, attacked Pearl Harbor. Soon after this, Germany declared war on the USA. Britain and the USA were now formal allies, but at this point in the war, their chances of defeating Germany appeared slim.

THE INVASION OF THE Soviet Union by the Nazis began in June 1941 when three million German soldiers poured across the border. But Soviet resistance proved more stubborn than the Germans had expected and the invasion led to the largest land battle in the history of the world. Despite staggering Soviet losses – some two million men within a matter of weeks – German forces were unable to capture Leningrad and Moscow and they were forced to camp outside the two cities for the winter.

By December 1941, Soviet losses amounted to four million men and the Germans had captured many of the country's vital food resources. Remarkably, the Soviets avoided a complete surrender. Their fierce, patriotic spirit led to extraordinary acts of determination and bravery. They physically moved whole factories eastwards to safety beyond the Ural Mountains and recruited new armies from distant parts of the Soviet Union.

While the Soviets bore the brunt of Nazi aggression on the eastern front, it became clear to many people in the West that if Britain and the USA could open a second front in western Europe it would relieve the pressure on Russia. Slogans began to appear on walls and railway arches in Britain calling for a 'Second Front Now'. The USA, keen to pursue the war against Japan but recognizing the need to defeat Germany first, wanted urgently to launch an invasion of northern Europe. As early as October 1940, while the Luftwaffe was still bombing London, Britain's wartime leader, Winston Churchill, had established a government group to plan an eventual return to Europe. Churchill and the US president, Franklin D Roosevelt, had met within weeks of Pearl Harbor and agreed to pool their military resources and plan together the future conduct of the war.

Although Churchill agreed in principle with plans to invade Europe, he did not see eye to eye with the USA when it came to when and where to launch the operation. Churchill felt that Britain should protect her traditional area of influence in the Mediterranean and the route through Egypt to her empire in Asia. In 1942, the USA reluctantly agreed to an invasion of North Africa knowing that, by devoting time and resources to this, they would rule out the possibility of invading France in 1943. Churchill went on to persuade the USA to join with Britain in attacking

Russian farmers dig traps to prevent the advance of the German tanks in December 1941.

German bombers over London during the Battle of Britain. The bombing of cities by enemy planes was carried out by both sides during the war.

Nazi Europe from the south, through Italy. But it was clear to the USA that the best military plan would be an invasion of northern France across the English Channel. From northern France the Allies could advance eastwards towards Germany. Throughout 1943 the Allies discussed and argued among themselves. It was not until August that the first agreement was made to land on the beaches in Normandy in 1944.

A Voice From the Front Line

"In May we moved closer to the coast, in the countryside around Caen. Already in May, even in April, we were expecting an invasion. It was the subject of daily conversation. It was known that the British troops were being trained for a large invasion. We read in the papers, the German papers and Swiss papers, that Stalin was urgently in need of another front.... I calculated that it would be in Normandy for the simple reason that we had been posted there. We sat there and thought, well, this is where it will be."

The recollections in 1944 of Helmut Liebeskind, aged 22, a soldier in the German army, quoted in Nothing Less Than Victory *by Russell Miller.*

American and British military leaders, fronted by Roosevelt (left) and Churchill, pose for the cameras in Casablanca, North Africa, in 1943.

A German U-boat under attack by US planes. German submarines posed a serious threat to Allied shipping in the Atlantic and elsewhere.

THE AGREEMENT BETWEEN the British and Americans to invade France in 1944 marked a new and closer partnership, one that would face severe strains and difficulties over the months ahead. There were unpredictable factors to consider, such as the crucial question of whether the Soviet Union could hold out against the German onslaught. If the Soviets were defeated, Germany could move men and resources to defend northern France and make an invasion there virtually impossible. The USA and Britain also needed to defeat the German submarines in the Atlantic Ocean to secure sea lanes for the transportation of men and equipment from the USA to England.

In planning the invasion of northern France, the Americans were more enthusiastic than the British. Meetings revealed differences of opinion that gave rise to heated discussions across the conference table. The British had good reason to fear the German military machine – they had already suffered a number of defeats in Europe. At the beginning of the war they had been driven out of Norway, then from France and Greece. The Americans felt that their allies were dragging their feet. At the end of 1943, matters came to a head when Churchill, Roosevelt and the Soviet leader, Stalin, met at a conference in Teheran.

Dwight D Eisenhower (1890–1969)

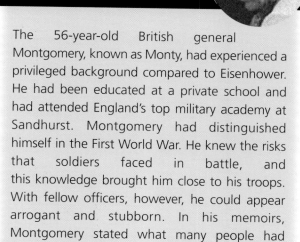

The 53-year-old American general, Eisenhower (known to everyone as Ike), had grown up in the US state of Kansas. His family was not wealthy, but he had attended West Point, a military school, and worked his way up through the army without experiencing an actual war. It was not until he was put in charge of the invasion of North Africa in 1942 that he first saw a dead soldier. Eisenhower's strengths lay in his exceptional organizational talent and his natural ability to get on with other people. Eisenhower explained that his idea of leadership was like 'pulling a piece of spaghetti across a plate, rather than trying to push it'. By this he meant that he preferred to involve and interest people rather than try to force them to do something against their will. His idea of leadership was put to the test when he encountered the British general, Montgomery.

Bernard Law Montgomery (1887–1976)

The 56-year-old British general Montgomery, known as Monty, had experienced a privileged background compared to Eisenhower. He had been educated at a private school and had attended England's top military academy at Sandhurst. Montgomery had distinguished himself in the First World War. He knew the risks that soldiers faced in battle, and this knowledge brought him close to his troops. With fellow officers, however, he could appear arrogant and stubborn. In his memoirs, Montgomery stated what many people had observed at the time: 'Ike and I were poles apart'.

At the Teheran conference, Stalin argued that an invasion of western Europe should take place as soon as possible, and he fully backed the Americans' insistence that Normandy be invaded in 1944. Stalin wanted agreement on a firm date and an overall commander for the operation. Roosevelt chose a United States general, Dwight D Eisenhower, as the Supreme Commander of the Allied Expeditionary Force; a British general, Bernard Law Montgomery, was chosen to command the ground forces once they landed in Normandy. The two men could not have been more different and they held varying opinions, not least on military matters, which added to the problems facing Britain and the USA.

Eisenhower, as the man in overall charge of D-Day, occupies the central seat at the table. Montgomery is on his left.

THE BRITISH AND AMERICAN invasion of northern France was to depart from ports in the south of England. For this to happen, all the American soldiers taking part had to be present in Britain before D-Day. Over the course of six months, some two million Americans and Canadians took up temporary residence in Britain, a country the size of the US state of Colorado. Their arrival had a tremendous impact on the lives of the British people, and the sudden bringing together of two cultures – despite their sharing a common language – was an education for both groups.

It soon became obvious that the ordinary American soldier, the GI, enjoyed much higher pay than his British counterpart (nearly five times as much, in fact). It also became apparent that the British

armed forces were far more divided by social class than the US army. While officers in the British army were made up of members of the middle and upper classes, the majority of ordinary soldiers were working class, and there was little social mixing between the two groups. By comparison, the American officers and ordinary soldiers seemed to mix freely with one another, and this came as a welcome surprise to a large number of British people.

Many of the Americans who poured into England during 1943 and early 1944 lived in special

In Britain, black US troops prepare for D-Day. The US army had a quota of no more than ten per cent of black soldiers, who were housed in separate units from the white US troops.

camps, but many also found themselves living with ordinary British families. Wherever they lived, when they were off duty, Americans socialized with the British and many friendships and relationships developed once they got to know one another. African-American GIs could not help but notice how they were treated better by the British than by their own army, which segregated them because of their colour. They did not know that the British authorities had asked the Americans not to send black troops nor that African soldiers were removed from French units destined to take part in D-Day so that only white troops would take part in the liberation of France.

By and large, Americans found the British people to be friendly and came to admire the way they were enduring the harshness of living through a war that had already killed 60,000 civilians. Many British people warmed to the informality of American manners and the generosity with which they shared provisions that were strictly rationed in Britain. One thing they all had in common was a dislike of the powdered eggs and dehydrated potatoes that people had no choice but to eat in wartime Britain. At times, of course, tensions did develop between the Americans and the British, summed up in a phrase that was to become a familiar complaint against the GIs: 'Over-paid, over-sexed and over here.'

GI Brides

" The Yanks were the most joyful thing that ever happened to British womanhood... they had everything – money in particular, glamour, boldness, cigarettes, chocolates, nylons, jeeps... countless British women who had virtually no experience in this line were completely bowled off their feet. It was astonishing how such vast quantities of women of all ages and stations fell for them. Apart from their Hollywood-style glamour, which they played to great effect, they were stupendously rich by the British serviceman's standards and could treat girls to things that were beyond the Britons' ability. "

In D-Day, by Juliet Gardiner, a British soldier, Eric Westman, explains how more than 80,000 British women would become GI brides by the end of the war. Is there a note of envy in his words?

Many romances and marriages occurred as the result of British women meeting GIs stationed in Britain.

Preparations for D-Day take place at a coastal town in southern England. In the foreground is a barrage balloon, used to protect shipping from low-flying air attack.

D-DAY WAS DESTINED TO be the largest and most complicated amphibious assault in the history of the world, and it took more than 350,000 men and women to plan it. The land operation was codenamed 'Overlord', and the naval operation was codenamed 'Neptune'.

To a great extent the success of both Neptune and Overlord depended on keeping secret from the Germans where and when the invasion would take place. The fact that two million men and many thousands of ships were being prepared for the operation made it seem highly likely that it would be found out. However, even though the Germans knew an invasion was to take place in 1944, they never discovered what the destination and date of D-Day were to be.

To fool the enemy, the Allies mounted an imaginary campaign – Operation 'Bodyguard' – which managed to convince the German command that Calais was to be the likely destination of an invasion force based in south-east England. A force of one million soldiers was invented and given the name of the First US Army Group. Information was deliberately fed to German intelligence to give the impression that this non-existent army was stationed in south-east England. Fake camps were created to house this imaginary force, and set designers from an English film studio created tanks made of rubber to make the deception more believable. In the south-west of England, from

Here women work to waterproof guns for the Normandy landings.

where the real attack on Normandy would depart, equally elaborate measures were taken to disguise the military build-up. Even khaki-coloured towels were used to replace the standard white towels used by the army to make them less conspicuous. Although it was impossible to keep the build-up of troops in south-west England completely secret, Hitler's reaction to the news of troop movements there was to assume that they were a diversion. The Germans thought that landings in Normandy were planned to draw their fire – the real landings, they believed, would take place at Calais.

The Allies knew that the Germans would demolish the harbours on the northern French coast. This was a huge problem: eight convoys of ships were to leave for

France every day throughout the invasion and harbour facilities were essential for unloading supplies and equipment. An imaginative solution was arrived at; artificial harbours would be transported across the Channel. Long concrete sections with their own floating piers would be towed by tugs, as part of the invasion fleet, to form harbours on the French coast. This plan was codenamed 'Mulberries', and the name also came to refer to the artificial harbours. More than fifty old ships and vessels were deliberately sunk further out at sea to make a breakwater to help protect the Mulberry harbours. This breakwater was known as 'Gooseberries'. Thousands of men and women welded the harbours and 10,000 men were used to tow them and set them in place on D-Day.

In Normandy, a partly constructed roadway will eventually link up with the pierhead in the distance. At the time of D-Day, men, supplies and equipment were unloaded by way of these artificial harbours.

A Moment in Time

In August 1942, six thousand soldiers, mostly Canadians, make a raid on the northern French coastal town of Dieppe. The raid is planned as a nine-hour operation: five hours ashore and four for withdrawal. It is a terrible disaster, mainly because the Germans have foreknowledge of the operation. Within three hours of landing a first wave of more than 500 men, over ninety per cent of them are casualties. Half the total number of troops are killed or captured on the beach before the evacuation is completed.

With the failure of the Dieppe raid in 1942 (see box above), the Allies learned that German fortifications in France were much stronger than they thought. It helped convince them that it was essential to undertake detailed planning and to assemble vast numbers of troops before mounting a large-scale invasion of northern France.

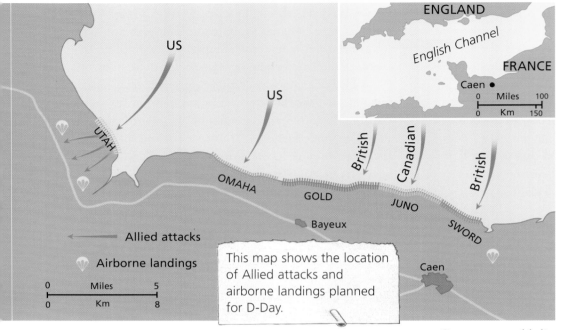

This map shows the location of Allied attacks and airborne landings planned for D-Day.

and 'Omaha', while the British and Canadians would land on the three beaches to the east, codenamed 'Gold', 'Sword' and 'Juno'. Twelve thousand aircraft would support the invasion, and paratroopers would land during the night prior to D-Day to knock out German lines of communication and defence. In Britain, troops began to move into transit camps and were not allowed to leave.

In the final weeks leading up to D-Day, there was a growing sense of tension. More than ever, there was concern that Germany would discover secret information about the invasion. An Australian journalist based in one of the camps in the south of England noticed how the atmosphere changed once the camp gates were locked and the soldiers knew that D-Day was near. The tension only broke, he said, when they were finally told that they would sail on 5 June.

As well as a general codename, military operations have a D-Day and an H-Hour, for the day and the time when the operation will begin. In May 1944, General Eisenhower confirmed that D-Day would be 5 June and that H-Hour would be 5.58 am.

15 May Eisenhower and Montgomery held a meeting of senior officers in London at which the final plans for the invasion were explained. American forces would land on the two most westerly beaches in Normandy, codenamed 'Utah'

25 May Final operational orders were sent to the captains of the ships. To maintain secrecy, all mail from American troops was suspended for ten days and all transatlantic communication lines were blocked.

On 5 June 1944, Eisenhower pays a last-minute visit to the paratroopers of the US 101st Airborne Division.

Guide books were issued to Allied soldiers. 'Don't be surprised if a Frenchman steps up to you and kisses you.... It means he's darned glad to see you!' read the American version.

28 May From this day onwards, soldiers began moving towards their embarkation points. Once in a port, no one was allowed to leave.

1 June Coded messages to begin disruptive action against German lines of communication were broadcast by the BBC to French Resistance groups.

3 June Eisenhower began to show signs of stress and developed a ringing in one ear. His ability to keep cool under pressure was severely tested when, on this day, the weather suddenly deteriorated.

4 June At 4 am Eisenhower met with his commanders, and the RAF's senior weatherman told them all what they most feared. Clouds would be hanging low over the Channel on 5 June, and a strong force six wind was expected. The whole operation was at risk because the sea would be too rough and aircraft would not have clear visibility. Eisenhower postponed D-Day until 6 June and ships that had already left British ports were called back. The nature and times of the tides meant that any delay beyond 6 June would involve postponing the whole operation for weeks. At such a late stage, this was unthinkable. At 9.15 pm another meeting took place.

The weatherman now believed that there could be a temporary break in the bad weather.

5 June At a meeting at 4.15 am, the weatherman felt more confident that conditions would improve. It was up to Eisenhower to make the decision. Everyone waited in silence. 'OK,' he said, 'let's go.' The invasion would take place on 6 June.

Suspense Over

"The change was electric. The suspense was snapped. A wave of relief succeeded it. Now the future was known and prescribed, everything would be easier.... As the men stood in their ranks listening to the colonel you could feel the confidence growing. Here at last was something practical and definite, something to which one could adjust oneself. "

Journalist Alan Moorehead remembers how the atmosphere in the camp in which he was staying changed when men heard that the final order for the invasion had been given.

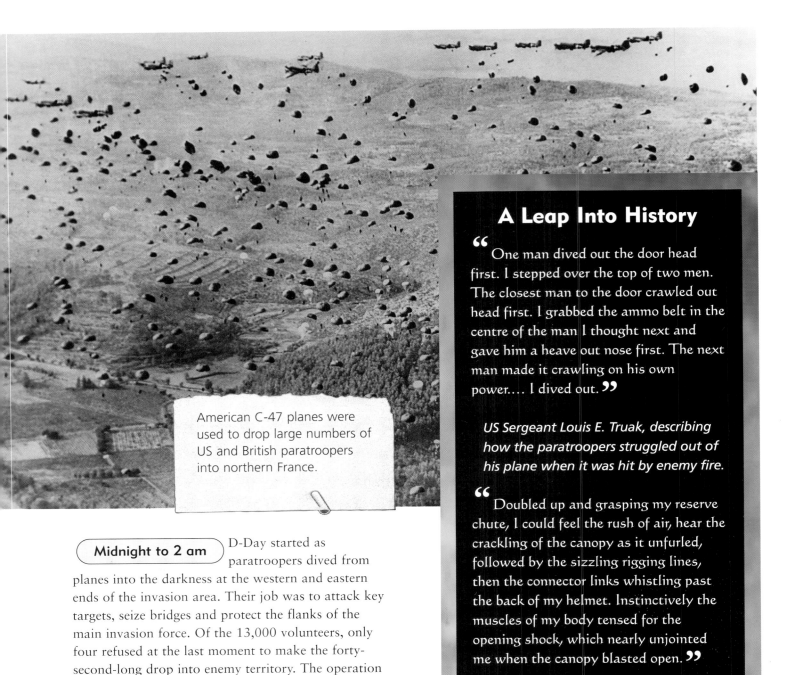

American C-47 planes were used to drop large numbers of US and British paratroopers into northern France.

A Leap Into History

" One man dived out the door head first. I stepped over the top of two men. The closest man to the door crawled out head first. I grabbed the ammo belt in the centre of the man I thought next and gave him a heave out nose first. The next man made it crawling on his own power.... I dived out. "

US Sergeant Louis E. Truak, describing how the paratroopers struggled out of his plane when it was hit by enemy fire.

" Doubled up and grasping my reserve chute, I could feel the rush of air, hear the crackling of the canopy as it unfurled, followed by the sizzling rigging lines, then the connector links whistling past the back of my helmet. Instinctively the muscles of my body tensed for the opening shock, which nearly unjointed me when the canopy blasted open. "

Donald Burgett, another US paratrooper, remembers the first few seconds of his jump. Both quotes from Six Armies in Normandy by John Keegan.

(Midnight to 2 am) D-Day started as paratroopers dived from planes into the darkness at the western and eastern ends of the invasion area. Their job was to attack key targets, seize bridges and protect the flanks of the main invasion force. Of the 13,000 volunteers, only four refused at the last moment to make the forty-second-long drop into enemy territory. The operation was not a complete success (mainly because of the pitch-dark conditions and pilots who were inexperienced at dealing with anti-aircraft fire) and the paratroopers found themselves scattered over a wide area. This confused the Germans, who found it difficult to assess what was happening, especially as thousands of dummies were also dropped by parachute to draw the enemy's fire.

3.00 am Some 2,000 Allied planes began a two-hour bombing raid on German installations and barracks near the landing area. Hundreds of tons of high explosive were dropped. German radar picked up signs of activity in the Channel.

3.30 am Two hours before first light, seventy-two gliders carrying heavy guns and equipment landed in France. Six gliders had landed earlier in the morning with the first paratroopers.

5.00 am The first warships made their appearance off the French coast and their guns began to pound the beach defences. French Resistance groups carried out acts of sabotage against the German communications system, such as the cutting of telephone and cable lines. By mid-morning, the first French civilian accused of collaboration was executed by the Germans. In total, eighty civilians would be executed for helping the invaders.

6.00 am By this point, the Channel had become crowded with the Allied invasion fleet, an armada of over 6,000 vessels including converted liners, merchant ships, mine-sweepers, landing craft, battleships and destroyers.

6.30 am The first American troops began to disembark on Utah and Omaha beaches on the western flank of the landing area.

US assault troops glimpse at the battle they are only moments away from joining as they approach the French coast.

Weighed down with equipment and weapons, Allied soldiers wade ashore.

5.45 am Two-thirds of the American forces were scheduled to land at Omaha beach, which was about 5 kilometres (3 miles) in length. At Omaha there was near disaster. The German bunkers above the beach had not been hit by Allied bombers, and their machine guns were all trained on the sand when the first wave of Americans landed. The cliffs at the top of the beach towered up to 60 metres (200 feet) in height, which made the advance extremely difficult for the disembarking soldiers. From the ships, the US troops had been bumped in landing craft through metre-high (four-foot) waves. In the shallows, ramps were lowered from the landing craft, down which the young men had to run through the surf and on to the beach. As they landed, the troops were cut down by continuous fire from the German bunkers. Those who managed to dodge the bullets scrambled desperately for cover by digging into the sand behind corpses and abandoned equipment. This first wave of troops had included specially trained demolition men, whose job it was to clear the beach of mines. But so many of them were killed that the beach became clogged with damaged and abandoned landing craft. A sprawling traffic jam developed off the beach.

6.30 am Utah, the most westerly of the beaches, had also been designated by the Allies for American troops. The landing here was remarkably successful and did not meet with fierce resistance, although soldiers found they had to struggle to cross an area of flooded fields beyond the beach. Of the 23,000 men who landed, there were only 197 casualties.

9.15 am The man in charge of the Omaha landing, General Bradley, considered abandoning the entire operation.

The Allied plan for D-Day depended to a degree on landing tanks. If successfully landed, the tanks would help the infantry through the enemy defences. But getting them on to the beaches and ready for immediate action presented a problem, as tanks are land machines and not suited to water. To overcome this obstacle, the DD (Duplex Drive) tank was specially adapted to operate in water and to land through its own power on the beach. The DDs had propellers and a canvas screen or 'skirt' that kept the water out. Once on land, the skirt collapsed and the tank could move forward and fire at enemy positions. Generally, the DDs were effective, but at Omaha the rough waves broke the canvas screens, especially of those tanks launched too far offshore. As a result, many of the DDs sank.

10.30 am   Some troops managed to reach a sea wall at the top of the beach and from there launched into close-quarter engagements with the enemy. They forced a path around the German strongholds, which became an escape route off the beach. By the end of the day they had established control of a road running inland, and vehicles were beginning to move. Of the 34,000 men who landed at Omaha, there were 2,500 dead or wounded within a few hours; by the end of the day, more than 1,000 men had died on the beach.

At Omaha, soldiers had to crawl up the beach under enemy fire.

At Utah, injured GIs are helped up the beach by their fellow soldiers.

The Horror

"Unseen snipers concealed in the cliffs were shooting down at individuals, causing screams from those being hit.... There were dead men floating in the water and there were live men acting dead, letting the tide take them in. I was crouched down to chin-deep in the water.... I don't know how long we were in the water before the move was made, but I would guess close to an hour.... I watched a GI get shot trying to cross the beach... and he screamed for a medic. One of the aid men moved quickly to help him and he was shot too. I'll never forget seeing that medic lying next to the wounded GI and both of them screaming. They both died within minutes."

Sergeant John R. Slaughter, aged nineteen on D-Day, remembers what he heard and saw when the ramp of his landing craft was lowered on Omaha beach.

British troops land successfully at Sword, and prepare to leave the beach.

7.00 – 7.30 am The first British troops landed on Sword and later on Gold beach. The German bunkers at Gold beach, like those at Omaha, had not been seriously damaged by bombardment from the air or sea, and the British troops landing there met with stiff resistance. Tanks were late in arriving and many men were killed on the sand within minutes of landing.

7.45 am Canadian troops landed on Juno beach, a few miles to the west of Sword. At Juno, landing was delayed by fifteen minutes, which meant the tide had come that much further in. A large number of the landing craft fell victim to the obstacles buried in the sand under the waves. The Germans had planted steel stakes, up to 1.8 metres (six feet) long, in the sea from high water mark. The stakes were doubly dangerous in that they were mined. The DD tanks were again late in landing and other tanks, which had not been adapted in the same way, were lost in large numbers. In one engagement, half of those men leading an assault over 90 metres (100 yards) were killed or injured.

8.55 am Within ninety minutes of landing at Sword, some British troops had advanced well over 1.6 kilometres (1 mile) inland. The British used a greater number of specially adapted tanks (known as the Funnies) than the Americans, and they proved effective in clearing the beaches. One type of tank had two arms fixed to its front, which supported a revolving drum. When the drum turned, short lengths of chain that were attached to it flew around and flailed the land, exploding mines before the tank reached them.

10.25 am British troops captured a German stronghold guarding Sword beach.

In total, 156,000 troops landed on the beaches of Normandy on D-Day, and around 2,500 were killed. Until that day, most of the soldiers had never experienced war or seen a dead body. They had to cope with these horrors and deal with the confusion of fast-unfolding events at the same time. One young engineer summed up what many soldiers probably felt as the day drew to a close: 'I was a cold, frightened, confused, terribly tired and hungry, not very brave young soldier.'

By the end of D-Day, the Allies had a foothold in Nazi Europe, but not much more than that. At Omaha, the Americans had only a toehold of control, and the British had failed in their plans to capture Caen. The final outcome of the events of D-Day, and whether they would prove successful, depended on how quickly and efficiently the Allies could consolidate their invasion and how rapidly the German army could respond to it.

Death on the Beach

" In the centre of the position was a huge concrete observation tower, an enormous thing with walls about three metres [ten feet], and some Germans who were at the top of it started firing at us. My signaller, who was just beside me, was shot and killed, and one of my subalterns [officer of lower rank], who had got up close to the tower, was killed when they dropped a grenade on him. He was a great friend of mine; I'd been best man at his wedding only two months before. He was trying to see if we could smoke them out. "

Patrick Porteous, quoted in Nothing Less Than Victory *by Russell Miller.*

Only after clearing the beach of all enemy positions could soldiers afford to relax.

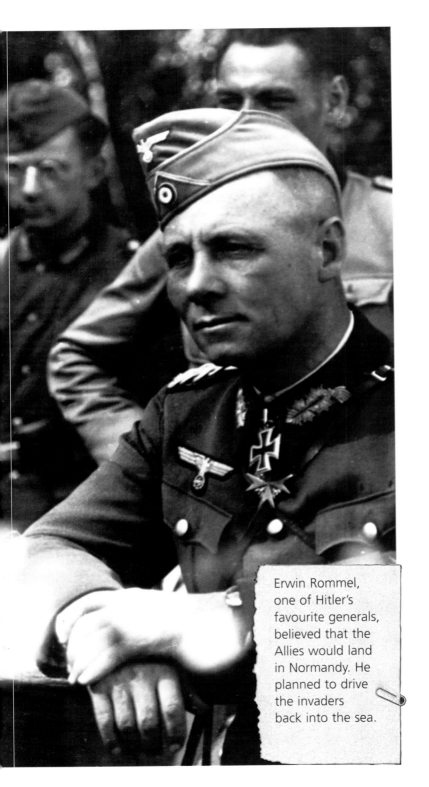

Erwin Rommel, one of Hitler's favourite generals, believed that the Allies would land in Normandy. He planned to drive the invaders back into the sea.

THE BAD WEATHER THAT preceded D-Day allowed the German commanders to relax their guard; they felt sure an invasion would not be launched at such a time. On 5 June, the regular naval patrols were cancelled. General Rommel, the officer in charge of repulsing the expected invasion, took a couple of days off and returned to Germany for his wife's birthday on 6 June. When news of the first Allied airborne landings reached the German command, it took some time for them to make sense of what was happening.

The German commanders could not be certain that Normandy was the main assault or whether this would take place later in the area around Calais. Rommel did not return to Normandy to direct the situation until late that afternoon.

At 10 am on 6 June, news of the Normandy landings reached Hitler's headquarters, but no one wanted to inform him until after breakfast. When he was told, Hitler appeared unconcerned; he believed that the main attack would be directed at Calais. It was not until late in the afternoon that he gave permission to move some reinforcements into Normandy. Rommel then ordered troops to the west of Caen and successfully blocked the British who were advancing on the city from Sword beach.

Allied supremacy in the air was of decisive importance on D-Day. Fortunately for the Allies, the Luftwaffe had been seriously weakened in the months before D-Day in air battles over Germany. At this point, the Luftwaffe could not muster much of a force against the Allies; had they been able to attack the invasion fleet and the beaches, it is likely that the D-Day landings would have failed. The German navy was similarly exhausted, and the Allied invasion was able to proceed without the serious threat of enemy attacks from the air or the sea.

The first German prisoners on D-Day. 'I didn't feel too bad about being captured and I was thankful to be alive,' wrote one young German.

Under Fire

" Ferdie said to me: 'You're the only one beside the battalion commander who's got a machine gun. You'll be the first out of here, believe me.' I said: 'No, I'm not going to do it,' and I pulled out the locking pin that held the machine gun together. Just then the man in the observation post shouted: 'My God, they're bringing up a flamethrower!'

We heard the 'woof' of the flame-thrower, but the flames couldn't get through the staggered sections of the ventilation shaft, although it turned red hot before our eyes... eventually we took one of the dirty white sheets from one of the wounded and, with the help of a broomstick, pushed it out through the observation hatch. "

Gefreite Joseph Haeger was nineteen years of age on D-Day. Guarding Juno beach with a machine-gun, he was forced to retreat with other soldiers, including his friend Ferdie. They found themselves in a bunker and under heavy fire from Canadian troops. The officer in charge ordered his men to attempt a break out, but the soldiers chose to surrender instead. Quoted in Nothing Less Than Victory *by Russell Miller.*

27

Allied forces move off the beaches and into France. As the Allies advanced inland, they met with stiff resistance from the German army.

By the end of 6 June, more than 150,000 Allied soldiers had landed successfully in Normandy, but the situation on each of the five beaches was quite different. At Utah, the Americans had pushed several kilometres inland and linked up with the airborne troops that had arrived earlier. At Omaha, however, the beach was only just held by the Allies, and a sense of crisis had persisted there throughout D-Day. At Gold beach, the British had pressed inland and formed a bridgehead nearly 5 kilometres (3 miles) wide and more than 3 kilometres (2 miles) deep. At Sword and Juno, troops were well-established off the beaches. The fact that the Allies had not been trapped on the beaches meant that 6 June was a success, and within twenty-four hours the possibility of Allied troops being pushed back into the sea was fading.

On 7 June, the Allies captured Bayeux, and American forces from Omaha met up with British troops advancing from Gold beach. Montgomery went ashore and set up his headquarters and Eisenhower crossed the Channel to observe the beaches from out at sea. Through binoculars, he could make out the lines of men and machines trailing away from the beaches and into the Normandy countryside of narrow roads and high hedgerows. It was difficult terrain to advance through at speed, and the Allies' slow progress suited the Germans. It was not until 10 June that patrols from Utah and Omaha beaches met one another and started to form a continuous front. Meanwhile, back on the beaches, fresh supplies of men and machines were pouring in. By 11 June, 320,000 men, more than 50,000 vehicles and 100,000 tons of supplies had been landed.

Northern France was bombed before, during and after D-Day. The Resistance also carried out bomb attacks to help the Allies.

Waiting For News

" The next day all my husband's letters that had been held up arrived. In one of them he begged me to keep writing. I wrote to him every day for three anxious weeks. Every day I waited for the postman to bring me that longed-for card. The card never came. Instead a letter arrived from the War Office telling me that it was their 'painful duty to inform me' that my husband had been killed on D-Day. "

The husband of Mrs F. Jones wrote to his wife every other day, but around D-Day the letters suddenly stopped. From D-Day by Juliet Gardiner.

Rommel was determined to hold back the British at Caen, a city of some 50,000 inhabitants, reasoning correctly that beyond the city the road lay open to Paris. Further German reinforcements were brought in, consisting of the best fighting troops in the world who had been hardened by experience in the Soviet Union and against the Americans and the British in Italy and elsewhere. Time, though, was not on Rommel's side, and Allied bombing and the work of the French Resistance slowed down the arrival of reinforcements. Two divisions of German troops, who had been shifted from the eastern front, found that it took longer to reach Normandy from Paris than it had taken them to travel to France from the Soviet Union.

Allied troops shelter in Caen, a city that was intended to be captured on D-Day itself. In the end it took more than a month for the Allies to capture Caen.

The Allies celebrate the capture of Cherbourg (left). Caen (right) was virtually destroyed by Allied bombers in July 1944. But the rubble provided the German army with valuable cover.

ON D-DAY, THE ALLIED losses were fewer than expected, but this was little comfort to the infantry soldiers who had to fight their way out of the invasion area. They soon came to realize that the Germans not only generally possessed better weapons, but were also better trained, and more experienced and self-disciplined than their own army. One US soldier, Frank Irgang, observed soberly: 'If they hadn't been fighting for five years before we got here and hadn't had a two-front war on their hands at that, we'd have had a hell of a time licking them. They've been hard enough, the way it is.'

By 17 June, more than half a million men had landed in Normandy. However, on 19 June a severe gale began to rage in the Channel and lasted for four days. The two artificial harbours, the Mulberries, were badly damaged, one beyond repair. The disruption to supplies and planning slowed down Allied troop movements and their grounded planes were unable to attack German positions. Rommel planned a counter-attack but this was hampered by the failure of reinforcements to appear on time. Even with the troops he did have, Rommel managed to defend Caen against another Allied assault. By 26 June, the

Americans had captured Cherbourg, but they too found it difficult to break through the German lines at Cherbourg and elsewhere. Knowing that they could not achieve victory, the German generals wanted to retreat but Hitler overruled them. It was not until 7 August that he finally released the troops stationed around Calais, the area in which he had expected the main invasion to take place. The troops from Calais were used to help hold back the Allies.

Eisenhower was concerned that a situation of stalemate was developing, and he urged his commanders to get a move on. On 25 July, the successful American break-out from their invasion area began, backed up by heavy bombing from Allied aircraft. This time, the American force moved at speed and widened its area of attack, advancing towards Caen as well as further eastwards. The Germans, dug in around Caen, were in danger of being surrounded. Hitler, however, insisted that they counter-attack and sent a new general, Walter Model, to take charge. By the middle of August, Model realized that the situation was hopeless and was finally given permission to withdraw. For the first time since the outbreak of the Second World War, German forces in western Europe fled before the enemy.

Alan Moorehead, a journalist accompanying the Allies, noted how 'in a blind instinct for self-preservation' the Germans were beginning to surrender or desert. 'There were no drugs for their wounded; no time to bury their dead', he observed.

D-Day had achieved its objective, and the battle for Normandy was over.

A Moment in Time

The patchwork of small fields, narrow lanes and high hedgerows that make up the Normandy country-side poses a problem for the large Sherman tanks that the Allies are using to break through German lines. Without space to move and turn, the tanks travel too slowly. A soldier from Tennessee, named Roberts, says: 'why don't we get some saw teeth and put them on the front of the tank and cut through these hedges?' While the other soldiers are amused by this idea, Roberts' sergeant thinks it is a good one, and the Allies begin to collect steel from German beach obstacles. Steel tusks, welded on to the front of the tanks 60 centimetres (2 feet) above the ground, make the vehicles capable of uprooting hedgerows and breaking through them across fields. Known as 'Rhinos', the specially adapted tanks prove highly successful and make a tremendous difference to the army's mobility.

The Allies had the fast and easily manoeuvrable Sherman tank, shown here equipped with an improvised plough to cut through hedgerows. But the Sherman could not match the firepower of the German Tiger tank.

The British leader Winston Churchill, smoking a cigar, is kept informed of Allied plans for the advance through France after D-Day. Montgomery is on the right (pointing).

BY THE MIDDLE OF August more than two million men and almost half a million vehicles had landed on the Normandy beaches. Some 240,000 Germans had been killed or wounded in Normandy and a further 200,000 were captured or missing. Of the Allied forces, more than 36,000 men had been killed and more than 16,000 aircrew had lost their lives in the skies over Normandy. For Hitler, Normandy had been one of the most critical battles between his country and the Allies, and his army had clung on with grim determination. When the Germans realized that they had finally lost the battle, their armies fled eastwards to cross the River Seine and retreat back to Germany. 'We are gaining ground rapidly,' a German soldier wrote home, 'but in the wrong direction.' By 25 August, American troops were only 96 kilometres (60 miles) from the German border and Model was left with a force one-tenth the size of Allied troop numbers.

The struggle for Normandy after D-Day was not the only battle Germany had to fight. Towards the end of June, Stalin launched an advance against Germany in the east. The Soviet Union had planned this to coincide with the battle for Normandy, and it was one of the few instances in the whole war where the

Allied troops liberated Paris on 25 August 1944. Here a French woman spits at the captured German soldiers. A US army jeep follows on behind.

Soviets, the USA and Britain worked together on a common plan of action. It would still take another nine months, though, before Germany finally surrendered – an indication of how difficult it was to defeat the Nazi war machine. Hitler always insisted on fighting to the death: on the eastern front, for example, the Germans shot a total of around 15,000 of their own men because they failed to live up to Hitler's expectations.

Most of the Allied troops who landed on the beaches of Normandy were not battle-hardened soldiers and they had to learn quickly if they were to survive. They lived with the constant risk of sudden death – from enemy bombardment, and from landmines and snipers – as they advanced eastwards towards Germany. Enemy snipers were regarded with fear and loathing and, if captured, were often killed. However, as an American soldier recalled: 'We had snipers of our own, skilled soldiers, picked for their intelligence and keen eyesight…. It always struck me as odd: the enemy snipers were unspeakable villains; our own were heroes.'

Mines

" By now I had gone through aerial bombing, artillery and mortar shelling, open combat, direct rifle and machine-gun firing, night patrolling, and ambush. Against all of this we had some kind of chance; against mines we had none. They were viciously, deadly, inhuman. They churned our guts…. Soon each of the line companies had lost men to mines, and the rest of us were afraid to walk anywhere. "

George Wilson was a member of the US army that marched across Normandy and France after D-Day. Here he expresses the deep fear felt by the infantry as they pursued the enemy. From Linderman, The World Within War.

GIs pose for a photograph with a Soviet female soldier. The two armies met in April 1945 at the River Elbe in Germany.

EVEN AFTER LOSING THE battle of Normandy, Hitler clung to the hope that the tensions between his enemies would eventually save him. The communist Soviet Union and the capitalist states of the USA and Britain had very different economic and social systems; if their alliance against Germany failed to hold, Hitler hoped to make a pact with one side or the other. If that happened, there was always the possibility that an almost-defeated Nazi Germany would still survive. Hitler also pinned his hopes on developments in weaponry, such as a deadly rocket-propelled missile known as the V-2. This missile travelled faster than the speed of sound and at such an altitude that it couldn't be intercepted, but its invention took place too late to change the outcome of the war. More importantly, for the Allies the end was now in sight, and they stuck together and focused their efforts on defeating Germany.

As the Soviet army advanced from the east into Poland, they liberated the death camps that the Nazis had operated in that country. Six million Jews had been systematically murdered in the camps' gas chambers, as had many gypsies, homosexuals and communists. Of the survivors that the Soviets found, many were starved, skeletal and close to death. American and British troops advancing into western Germany also found scenes of unbelievable horror when they liberated concentration camps such as Bergen-Belsen and Buchenwald in April 1945.

The Second World War finally came to an end in September 1945, following the American assault on two Japanese cities – Hiroshima and Nagasaki – with a lethal new weapon, the atom bomb. For the combat soldiers who had landed on the beaches of Normandy, the war had ended four months earlier when German forces had formally surrendered in May 1945. The men who took part in the D-Day landings had experienced all the savagery of war. One American division, in which men were killed as quickly as they could be replaced, not only lost all its officers and men within six weeks but also fifty per cent of the reinforcements sent in to make up for those killed.

'Every face seemed older than it should have been, more hard-bitten,' observed the journalist George Hunt, who journeyed with troops across Europe. Many soldiers suffered nervous breakdowns in the long campaign that followed D-Day, and for some there came the realization that the men they were trying to kill were just like them in many ways. One artilleryman said: 'We recognized that we were in a war, but we recognized that German soldiers came from families like we came from and that they had loved ones…. Personally, I had no malice at any time towards the Germans.' At the same time, though, there is evidence that American soldiers preparing for D-Day were told by high-ranking officers to 'take no prisoners', in other words to kill them if they could.

A formal surrender of German forces took place on 7 May 1945 in the French city of Reims.

A Changed Man

" Thinking about it all now, I don't think he ever really got back to his old self. The war did something to him, apart from giving him an ulcer. His political views had changed somewhat. Also, he flatly refused to accept his medals and, when they arrived, he sent them straight back with a curt note. "

Although Elsie Moyer was reunited with her husband when he returned from Europe in 1945, she was shocked to discover the way in which war had affected him. From Welcome Home *by Ben Wicks.*

For these happy British servicemen, the ordeal of D-Day and the Second World War is over. Their next challenge will be the return to civilian life.

There was no red flag available when a Russian photographer wanted this shot of the German parliament building in Berlin in 1945. So he had three red tablecloths sewn together and added a hammer and sickle. He also airbrushed out one of the two watches being worn by the soldier at the bottom of the photo to disguise the fact that they had been obtained through looting.

THE ALLIANCE BETWEEN THE Soviet Union, the USA and Britain had held together and defeated Nazi Germany. Hitler's expectation that such a union would eventually dissolve was not unreasonable – there were deep differences of opinion between the Allies. The Soviet Union was a communist state opposed to capitalism, and it rejected the idea that society should be centred on the pursuit of profit through business. The USA and Britain believed in the 'free market' and were opposed to communism. Before the beginning of the war in 1939, relations between the Allies had not been good. Although the need to defeat Germany had brought them together, even then there was little co-operation between them.

As the war drew to a close, and the defeat of Germany became inevitable, the differences between the Allies began to emerge. Churchill urged Eisenhower to advance quickly into eastern Germany and seize Berlin before the Soviets did. The growing political conflict between the USA and the Soviet Union became known as the Cold War. The defeated Germany was divided along military lines between the American, British, Soviet and French armies. The city of Berlin itself was also divided between the Allies. Suspicions increased between the West (Britain and the United States) and the Soviet Union when it became obvious that they each wanted to preserve their opposing social and economic systems in Europe. Eastern Europe came under Soviet influence and western

A Moment in Time

After the Second World War, the US government becomes concerned that many German scientists, who during the war furthered the Nazi defence programme, may start to work for the Soviet Union. In the spring of 1946, a scheme is hatched to bring eminent German scientists to the USA. Called Operation Paperclip, it involves altering the files of Germans wanted for war crimes so that they appear innocent to the US immigration authorities. In the ten years following the war, more than 750 German scientists are brought to the USA. At least three-quarters of them are either ex-members of the SS (a Nazi police force) or the Nazi Party.

After the Second World War, food, resources and materials poured into western Europe from the USA under the Marshall Plan.

Europe came under the influence of the USA. Churchill called for a 'special relationship' between Britain and the USA, partly because of the close relationship that planning D-Day had brought about between the two countries and partly because they were now both opposed to the Soviet Union.

Russia had twice faced invasion from western Europe during the course of the twentieth century, and this time Stalin wanted control over Poland so that it would act as a buffer state. The USA wanted to prevent western Europe from falling under Soviet influence, especially France and Italy where there were large and active communist groups. The best way to achieve this was by restoring economic health to western Europe, and the USA invested many billions of dollars in European countries after the war in what became known as the 'Marshall Plan'.

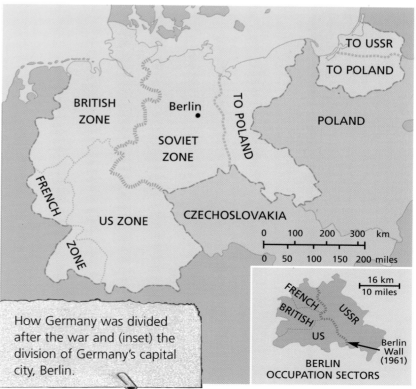

How Germany was divided after the war and (inset) the division of Germany's capital city, Berlin.

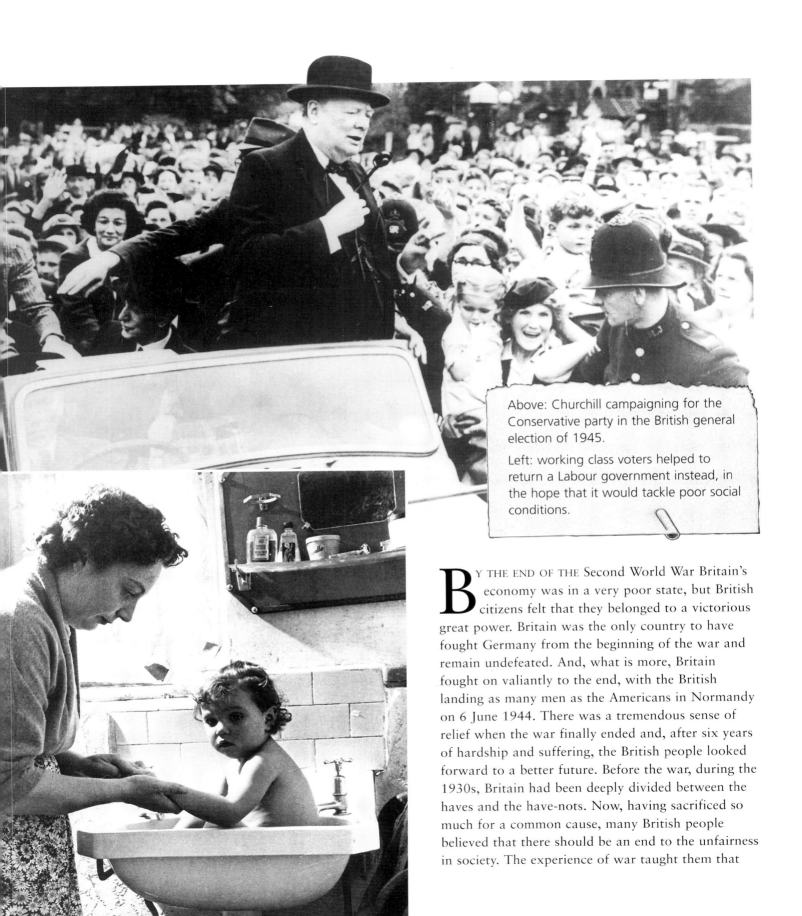

Above: Churchill campaigning for the Conservative party in the British general election of 1945.

Left: working class voters helped to return a Labour government instead, in the hope that it would tackle poor social conditions.

BY THE END OF THE Second World War Britain's economy was in a very poor state, but British citizens felt that they belonged to a victorious great power. Britain was the only country to have fought Germany from the beginning of the war and remain undefeated. And, what is more, Britain fought on valiantly to the end, with the British landing as many men as the Americans in Normandy on 6 June 1944. There was a tremendous sense of relief when the war finally ended and, after six years of hardship and suffering, the British people looked forward to a better future. Before the war, during the 1930s, Britain had been deeply divided between the haves and the have-nots. Now, having sacrificed so much for a common cause, many British people believed that there should be an end to the unfairness in society. The experience of war taught them that

The US economy was stronger than ever after the Second World War, and American families enjoyed a period of increasing prosperity.

the way they lived could be different. The new feeling in British society was expressed in the country's general election in 1945. A socialist Labour government gained power with a large majority, and it promised to build a more equal society through new, publicly-owned organizations such as the National Health Service. Although Churchill had been greatly admired as a war leader, he was also leader of the Conservative Party, and the Conservatives were generally believed to oppose the interests of working-class voters. People also remembered that the Conservative Party had failed to stand up to Hitler until war became inevitable.

The USA was also changed by the war, although in a very different way. The preparations for D-Day and for the defeat of Japan had transformed the American economy. By 1945, the USA was responsible for half the manufacturing output of the whole world and the country owned two-thirds of the world's gold. Before the war, the USA had not been a major military power but, by the time of D-Day, the country had a vast war machine that included over a thousand large warships and a huge army of trained soldiers. Britain's years as a world power were numbered, and the USA began to emerge as a global military power.

The Changing Role of Women

" Sheer physical effort plus wartime rations did wonders for my figure, but my fair hands assumed the look of leather. I enjoyed all of it. The big thing it did for me and many more women was to open a whole new world to us. We realized there were so many things we could do, long before the words women's lib were uttered.... Before I was born, my mother worked on the railway during World War I and then went back to the same old grind. Not for my generation. We looked for more and went for it. "

Muriel Hargeaves became an electrician during the Second World War, taking on a job that would normally have been assigned to a man. From Welcome Home *by Ben Wicks.*

In 1961 a wall was built across the German city of Berlin. It separated the Soviet-controlled east of the city from the pro-American west. This visible sign of the Cold War was demolished in November 1989.

IN DECEMBER 1943 HITLER said: 'If they attack in the west, that attack will decide the war'. The German leader was right. If German forces could have halted the invasion on the beaches of Normandy it would have taken a long time, years perhaps, before the Allies were able to make a second attempt. In the meantime, fifty divisions of the German army – and each division consisted of around 15,000 men – would have been transferred from northern France to the eastern front to take on the USSR. If the battle in the east had been won, and the weapons that German scientists were developing had continued to improve, the war would not have ended when it did. Two months after D-Day, the USA was ready to use the newly developed atomic bomb. If D-Day had failed, the use of such a weapon against Germany might have

been considered, but whether it would have been used in Europe can only be guessed at.

The success of D-Day was a decisive event that brought about the complete defeat of Nazi Germany. The final battles took place in Germany in 1945, but they could not have taken place unless there had been a successful outcome to the events of 6 June 1944. The Americans and the British who occupied the western part of Germany and the western half of its capital, Berlin, were mostly soldiers who had landed on the Normandy beaches from the 6 June onwards. For the next half century, Europe was divided into a pro-American western half and a Soviet-dominated eastern half and millions of people were subjected to the icy blast of the Cold War. During these years the

Fifty years after D-Day, representatives of the German, French and British governments work together at the European Parliament.

threat of war was ever present, until the Cold War came to a peaceful end between 1986 and 1991.

D-Day triggered the liberation of Europe from Nazism by opposing the German army with a combined American and British army. The Cold War created a divided Europe with the rival armies of the USSR and American-led NATO (North Atlantic Treaty Organization) facing each other across the continent. Europe had failed to find a lasting peace. The idea of a united Europe lay behind the Treaty of Rome in 1958 and the establishment of the EEC (European Economic Community), the organization that became the EU (European Union) in 1992. A united Europe, in which nationalist pride took second place to pride in a common identity, would reduce the risk of another war.

No More Wars in Europe?

" The objectives of the common foreign and security policy shall be:

- to safeguard the common values, fundamental interests and independence of the Union;

- to strengthen the security of the Union and its Member States in all ways;

- to preserve peace and strengthen international security, in accordance with the principles of the United Nations Charter as well as the principles of the Helsinki Final Act and the objectives of the Paris Charter;

- to promote international co-operation;

- to develop and consolidate democracy and the rule of law, and respect for human rights and fundamental freedoms. "

From the Maastricht Treaty on European Union, 1992, Article J.1.2.

Along the Normandy coast today there are memorials to those who died at D-Day. This monument to the soldiers stands at Utah beach.

D-DAY WAS JUST ONE day in a war that killed an average of 25,000 people every day for six years. Most of the slaughter of the Second World War took place in eastern Europe, the USSR and in Asia. For every American killed, eighty-five Soviet citizens died. D-Day was, however, a decisive event in world history because the success of this single operation meant that Hitler's days were numbered. D-Day started a new chapter in the history of Europe, which would take shape around the new world powers of the USA and the USSR.

Another important fact about D-Day is that it could so easily have ended in failure. And, despite all the careful planning and preparation, it came perilously close. Forty-eight hours before D-Day was supposed to start, Eisenhower postponed the operation because

the weather had suddenly changed. If he had waited until later in June, when the tides would again have been favourable, the invasion force would have been caught up in a far fiercer storm. When the landings did take place on 6 June, Eisenhower had a note in his wallet on which he had written an announcement concerning the failure of Operation Overlord – failure was always a possibility.

The outcome of D-Day was a close call. The German troops waiting in France for the invasion were better trained and more disciplined than the American, British and Canadian soldiers, or the small number of French and other nationalities who took part. The battle-hardened Germans had superior weaponry. D-Day owed much of its success to Operation Bodyguard, which convinced the German command that the real invasion force would land at Calais, not at Normandy. Hitler had an army waiting in Calais and if, at any time in the first few weeks after 6 June these troops had been moved to Normandy, the outcome could have been very different.

A great deal was at stake on 6 June 1944. Europe was ruled by a powerful Nazi state and, until the success of D-Day, its future lay in the balance. World events might have taken a different course, but D-Day determined that Hitler would be defeated in Germany. Without the success of D-Day, the Nazi dream of a new European civilization based upon racist principles might not have come to an end.

Hearing the News

" It was a stocking factory, turned over to making jettison fuel tanks for aircraft, and all the workers were women; and almost all of them had a son or a husband or a lover who had not told her for months what he was doing and had not written at all for weeks. Work stopped for a bit, and then went on with extra energy. Almost everyone in the factory was in tears. Connie Bowes kept her feelings to herself, but she wondered what Ivor was doing. "

Ivor Stevens landed at Sword beach on 6 June. His fiancée, Connie Bowes, was at work in a factory when news came over the radio that D-Day had begun. From Dawn of D-Day *by David Howarth.*

In 1994, on the fiftieth anniversary of D-Day, veterans of that momentous event were welcomed back to commemorate it in Normandy. The caption on the poster below reads: 'In June '44 we said "Thank you." In June '94 we say "Welcome".'

En juin 44, on leur a dit "thank you"
En juin 94, dites-leur "welcome".

CONSEIL REGIONAL BASSE-NORMANDIE

Glossary

Allies The countries at war against Germany, Japan and their supporters.

amphibious Operating on land and in water.

anti-aircraft fire Gunfire directed at enemy aircraft.

armada A large fleet of ships and/or boats.

artillery Large guns used in warfare on land.

atom bomb A hugely destructive bomb triggered by the splitting of atoms.

battleship The largest and most heavily-armed type of warship.

breakwater A huge wall built out into the sea to protect a shore or harbour from the force of waves.

bridgehead A position that is held on the enemy's side of a river or other obstacle.

buffer state A small state situated between two larger states, whose existence reduces the risk of hostility between the larger states.

bunkers Underground shelters.

capitalism An economic system based on private ownership and the pursuit of profits.

collaboration To work with others; to co-operate as a traitor with an enemy occupying one's own country.

communism An economic system based on public ownership of the means of production.

DDs Duplex tanks, specially adapted to move through water over short distances.

dictatorship A state ruled by a person with unrestricted authority.

fascist A form of government and a way of thinking that favours obedience to authority and the crushing of opposition with the force of state power.

flak Anti-aircraft fire.

flank The right or left side of a body of troops.

free market An economy where prices and wages are determined by competition.

French Resistance A group of French people who actively worked against the German occupation of their country during the Second World War.

front In a military setting, the front is the line of battle.

Funnies Tanks specially adapted for the purpose of landing during D-Day.

GI A private soldier in the US Army; GI is an abbreviation of government (or general) issue.

H-Hour Military codename for the particular time fixed for the beginning of an operation.

infantry Soldiers who fight on foot using rifles and other small arms.

installations Buildings serving a technical operation.

landmines Explosive devices buried just under the surface of the ground.

Luftwaffe The German airforce.

Nazi Hitler's National Socialist German Workers' Party, which governed Germany from 1933 to 1945.

Overlord The codename for the planned invasion of Normandy.

paratroopers Troops trained to be dropped by parachute into a battle area.

RAF The Royal Air Force; the airforce of Britain.

Russia The leading power and the largest union republic in the Union of Soviet Socialist Republics (USSR).

sea wall A wall or embankment designed to hold back the sea.

Sherman A reliable tank used more widely than any other Allied armoured vehicle.

snipers Riflemen firing at selected targets from hidden positions.

socialist Someone who opposes capitalism and usually believes in the public ownership of key industries and services.

Soviet Union A country formed from the territories of the Russian Empire after the Russian revolution of 1917. The Soviet Union was dismantled in 1991.

stalemate A standstill situation in which neither side can win an outright victory.

stronghold A strongly defended position.

superpower A world power, such as the USA, that can exert influence over smaller, less powerful countries.

transit camps Camps providing temporary accommodation for people who are expected to move elsewhere.

USSR The Union of Soviet Socialist Republics (also known as the Soviet Union).

Visit www.learn.co.uk for more resources.

Further Information

Reading

Allied Victory by Sean Sheehan (Hodder Wayland, 2000). Examines the course of events of the Second World War which led to the final success of the Allies.

D-Day by Juliet Gardiner (Collins & Brown, 1994). Photographs and eyewitness accounts by people who took part in D-Day.

D-Day by Anthony Kemp (Thames & Hudson, 1994). Photographs on every page telling the story of what happened from 6 June to the break-out from Normandy in July 1944.

Dawn of D-Day by David Howarth (Greenhill Books, 2001). Interesting account of D-Day, written in 1959, based on interviews with those who took part.

Eclipse by Alan Moorehead (Granta, 2000) Account of the last years of the war, including D-Day, by a journalist who arrived in Europe with troops in June 1944.

The Era of the Second World War by Neil De Marco (OUP, 1993). Investigating history at Key Stage 3.

Websites

Enter D-Day in your search program for a list of possible sites. Useful sites are:

http://www.normandy.eb.com/
The Encyclopaedia Britannica site on D-Day.

http://www.unverse.com/WW2.html
A Second World War site with section on D-Day.

http://www.militaryhistoryonline.com/wwii/dday/
Detailed accounts of D-Day and sections on events at each of the five beaches.

http://www.d-dayheadlines.com/
1944 newspaper headlines and stories about D-Day.

http://www.iwm.org.uk/
Imperial War Museum site – enter D-Day in the search index.

Places to visit

The Imperial War Museum in London has information on D-Day and a shop selling material suitable for projects. There are also museums close to the Normandy beaches, which are open to visitors.

Timeline

1939 Germany invades Poland; Britain and France declare war on Germany.

April to June 1940 Germany conquers Denmark, Norway, the Netherlands, Luxembourg, Belgium and France. British troops evacuated from Dunkirk in northern France.

22 June 1941 Germany begins an invasion of the Soviet Union but is halted outside Moscow in November.

7 December 1941 The Japanese attack Pearl Harbor.

8 December 1941 USA declares war on Japan.

11 December 1941 Germany declares war on the USA.

26 January 1942 The first US soldiers arrive in Britain.

June 1942 Eisenhower arrives in London as Commander of the US forces in Europe.

August 1942 An exercise landing at Dieppe in northern France proves a terrible failure.

August 1943 Plans for the invasion of Europe are approved by American and British leaders.

December 1943 Roosevelt, Churchill and Stalin meet at the Teheran Conference.

January 1944 The counties of southern England begin to fill with military camps for the invasion force.

6 June 1944 The invasion of Europe begins on the beaches of Normandy in northern France.

25 July 1944 The Allied break-out from the area of the Normandy beaches begins.

25 August 1944 Allied troops enter Paris.

May 1945 Germany surrenders to the Allies.

July 1945 Berlin is divided into Soviet and Western areas of control.

May to October 1949 Soviet occupation zone of Germany becomes East Germany and the zones under American, British and French control become West Germany.

1961 The Berlin Wall is built to divide the Soviet sector of the city from the Western sectors.

1989-1991 The Berlin Wall is torn down in 1989 and the Soviet Union breaks up and ceases to exist by the end of 1991. The Cold War is over.

1992 The Maastricht Treaty on the European Union proposes a common foreign and security policy for all member states.

Christian and Jewish graves lie side by side at a war cemetery in France.

Index